Push and Pull

By Patricia J. Murphy

Consultants
Martha Walsh, Reading Specialist

Jan Jenner, Ph.D.

Children's Press®
A Division of Scholastic Inc.
New York   Toronto   London   Auckland   Sydney
Mexico City   New Delhi   Hong Kong
Danbury, Connecticut

Designer: Herman Adler Design
Photo Researcher: Caroline Anderson
The photo on the cover shows children pushing and pulling a sled through the snow.

Library of Congress Cataloging-in-Publication Data

Murphy, Patricia J.
    Push and pull / by Patricia J. Murphy.
        p. cm. — (Rookie read-about science)
    Includes index.
    Summary: Simple text and photographs describe and illustrate push and pull movement.
        ISBN 0-516-22551-0 (lib. bdg.)   0-516-26864-3 (pbk.)
        1. Force and energy—Juvenile literature. [1. Force and energy.]
    I. Title. II. Series.
    QC73.4 .M87   2002
    531'.6—dc21

                                                                2001002686

Move it!

All objects need a push or a pull to start moving.

Elevator buttons need a push to make the elevator go up or down.

A swing needs a push to
fly high in the sky.

Your heart pushes blood through your body. This pushing keeps you alive.

Your muscles push your bones so you can move.

Can you think of other
things that need a push?

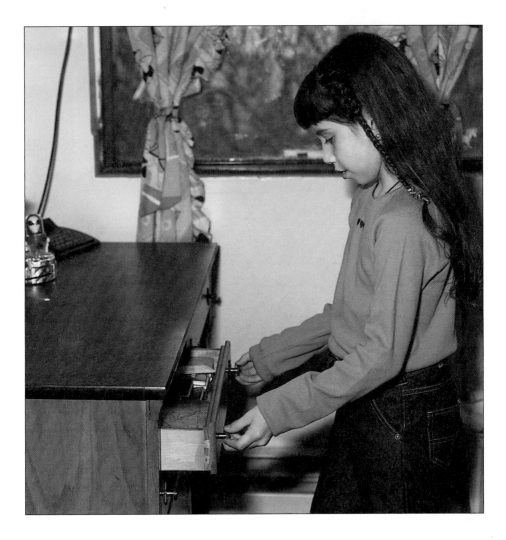

What about a pull?

A shoelace needs a pull
so you can take off
your sneaker.

A zipper needs a pull
to close your jacket.

Firemen and lifeguards pull people out of danger.

Cranes and tow trucks
pull heavy loads.

The pull of gravity (GRAV-uh-tee) keeps us on Earth. Without it, we would be floating in air.

YOU push and pull things all day long.

Waves pull things out to sea.

Sunshine helps young
plants push their way
up through the soil.

All of these objects
will keep moving until
something stops them.

Scientists call this inertia
(in-UR-shuh).

When moving objects meet a force called friction (FRIK-shuhn), they slow down or stop.

Friction happens when objects rub together.

When you push a marble off a table and it lands on the carpet, the marble rubs against the carpet.

This friction causes the marble to stop.

A "stopped" object will
not start moving again
until another force helps it.

It will need another push
or a pull!

Words You Know

crane   gravity

moving

pull

push

stop

31

Index

About the Author

Patricia J. Murphy lives in Northbrook, IL , where she writes children's books. She also writes for magazines, corporations, and museums. She loves to push and pull her nephew, Erik, in a swing, so he can fly high in the sky.

Photo Credits

Photographs © 2002: Corbis-Bettmann: 28 (Kelly-Mooney Photography), 24; Peter Arnold Inc.: 21 (David Cavagnaro), 5, 31 top left (Martha Cooper), 12 (Laura Dwight); Photodisc, Inc.: 6, 23, 31 bottom right; PhotoEdit: 20 (Bachmann), cover (Barbara Stitzer); Rigoberto Quinteros: 10, 11, 13, 17, 27, 30 right, 31 bottom left, 31 top right; Stone/Getty Images: 15, 30 left (Sandra Baker), 18 (Frank Siteman); The Image Works: 3 (B. Daemmrich), 14 (Mike Waters/Syracuse Newspapers); Visuals Unlimited: 8 (Gregg Ozzo), 7 (D. Yeske).